Whales for Kids

by Tom Wolpert
illustrated by John F. McGee

NORTHWORD PRESS

Minnetonka, Minnesota

WILDLIFE *For Kids* **SERIES** ™

Photography © 2000: Michael S. Nolan/Innerspace Visions: cover; Doug Perrine/Innerspace Visions: pp. 3, 9, 16-17, 45, 46-47; François Gohier: pp. 4, 20-21, 22, 29; David B. Fleetham/Innerspace Visions: pp. 6-7; Hiroya Minakuchi/Innerspace Visions: p. 10; John K. B. Ford/Ursus Photography: p. 13; Rich Kirchner: p. 14; Paul Nicklen/Ursus Photography: p. 19; Phillip Colla/Innerspace Visions: pp. 26-27; Brent Houston/The Green Agency: pp. 32-33; Marilyn Kazmers/Innerspace Visions: p. 37; James D. Watt/Innerspace Visions: p. 38; Brandon D. Cole: p. 41; Glen Williams/Ursus Photography: p. 42; Brandon D. Cole/Innerspace Visions: back cover.

NorthWord Press
5900 Green Oak Drive
Minnetonka, MN 55343
1-800-328-3895

Illustrations by John F. McGee / Book design by Russell S. Kuepper

National Wildlife Federation® is the nation's largest conservation, education and advocacy organization. Since 1936, NWF has educated people from all walks of life to protect nature, wildlife and the world we all share.

Ranger Rick® is an exciting magazine published monthly by National Wildlife Federation®, about wildlife, nature and the environment for kids ages 7 to 12. For more information about how to subscribe to this magazine, write: National Wildlife Federation, 8925 Leesburg Pike, Vienna, Virginia 22184.

NWF's World Wide Web Site www.nwf.org provides instant computer access to information about National Wildlife Federation, conservation issues and ideas for getting involved in protecting our world.

ISBN 0-55971-727-0

Printed in Malaysia
10 9 8 7 6 5 4 3 2

Whales for Kids

Humpback whale flukes are very powerful.

by Tom Wolpert
illustrated by John F. McGee

There are 76 species of whales swimming the oceans of the world today. Some dive to great depths and swim thousands of miles. Some are the largest animals that ever lived.

The blue whale, for instance, may grow 110 feet long and weigh 300,000 pounds. In fact, a brontosaurus, an elephant, and a human could fit on a blue whale's back with room to spare.

The fin whale has two blowholes, which can make a large spout.

Pages 6 and 7: The blue whale is the largest whale and is found in all oceans of the world.

Whales may look somewhat like fish, but they are not fish at all. Whales are mammals—just like dogs, cats, cows, and human beings.

Because they are mammals, whales give birth to live young (fish lay eggs). Baby whales nurse on their mother's milk for the first 6 months of their life (young fish do not nurse at all). Whales breathe through lungs and must hold their breath underwater (fish breathe through gills).

Like all whale parents, these humpbacks are keeping close guard of their calf.

But whales are also very different from most mammals.

For example, compare yourself to a whale. You can smell with your nose (a whale has no sense of smell). You hear with ears (a whale can hear but has no real ears, only tiny ear openings). You have 4 limbs–2 legs and 2 arms (a whale has only 2 front limbs called flippers).

So, even though humans and whales are both mammals, they are very different from one another.

The right whale is usually a slow swimmer, but it can jump high out of the water, showing its white belly.

Some types of whales feed and travel in groups that may number in the hundreds. These large groups are called herds or pods. Other whales travel in small family groups of 2 or 3 animals.

In the summer, whales migrate to cooler waters to feed. Then they travel back to warmer waters in the winter to give birth. A family group may include a bull (an adult male), a cow (an adult female), and a calf (a baby or immature whale).

This pod of beluga whales is migrating to the cooler waters of the Arctic Ocean.

Female whales carry their young inside their bodies for up to 18 months before giving birth. When born, calves do not have enough blubber, or fat, to float. Mother whales constantly bring their babies to the surface to help them breathe.

After 1 month, calves have enough blubber to float and swim without help. They play and learn to turn, roll, and dive. If a calf is too playful the mother hugs it against her belly with her flippers until it calms down.

This baby gray whale is being lifted to the surface on its mother's back.

Pages 16 and 17: This sperm whale calf seems tiny compared to its parent, but it is learning many things by staying near.

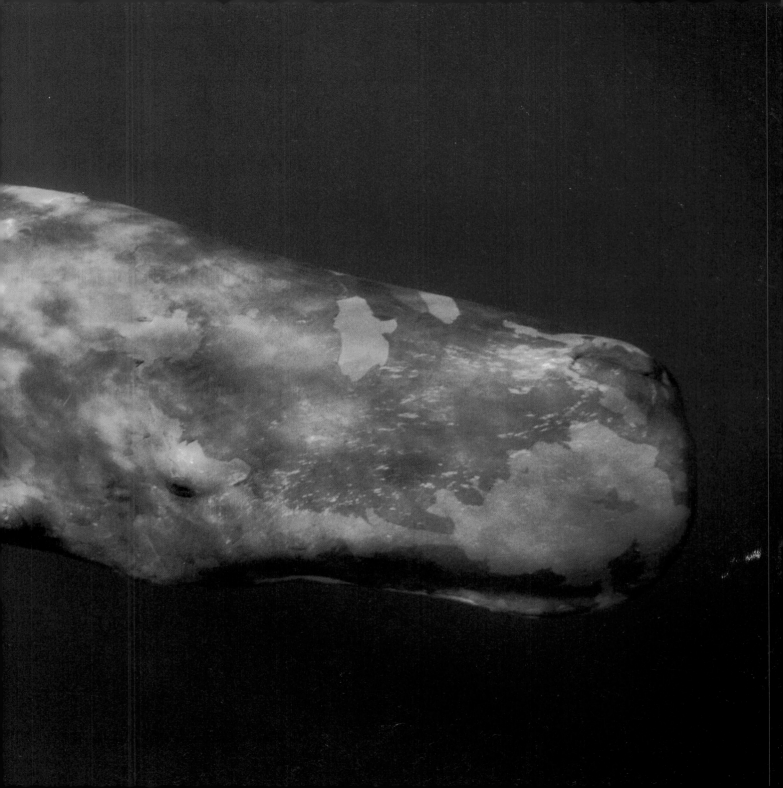

Whales swim by thrusting their powerful tail fins up and down. These fins are called flukes. Their flippers are used only for balance and turning. Many whales also have a dorsal fin on their back. It helps them swim without rolling over. Most whales swim at a speed of 3 to 5 miles per hour. However, blue and killer whales can go as fast as 25 miles per hour!

Pages 20 and 21: Humpbacks often "breach," or jump out of the water. Sometimes more than one jumps at the same time.

As this bowhead whale dives back into the water, its flukes are the last thing we see.

Adult whales use their size and power to protect their young. Whales have only one enemy other than man. That enemy is the killer whale. Whales do not, as far as we know, fight among themselves, and whales seldom attack boats unless they have been wounded.

Whales swim and dive most of the time. To protect their eyes from the salty ocean water, whales produce an oily substance that covers them.

Whales depend on their sense of hearing more than on their sense of sight. Whales do not sleep for long periods of time but take naps for a few minutes at a time at the surface of the water.

Killer whales, or "orcas," usually have about 45 teeth, for eating their main diet of fish and squid.

Even though whales breathe air, they would die on land. If a whale is stranded on land, the great weight of its body presses down on its lungs and the whale suffocates. It needs the water to support the weight of its huge body.

Whales have pretty big appetites! Larger whales may eat nearly a ton of food daily.

When whales dive for food, the air in their lungs becomes hot and moist from body heat. At the surface, they blow the air out through 1 or 2 holes in the top of their head. The hot breath strikes the cold air outside and forms a spout of fog.

Those fog spouts, or "blows," can spray as high as 15 feet in the air. They can be seen from great distances. Most people wish only to observe the gentle, friendly whales. Others, however, are commercial hunters who kill whales for their meat, hide, and body oil.

Pages 26 and 27: The fin whale has a slender body, but can weigh up to 100 tons.

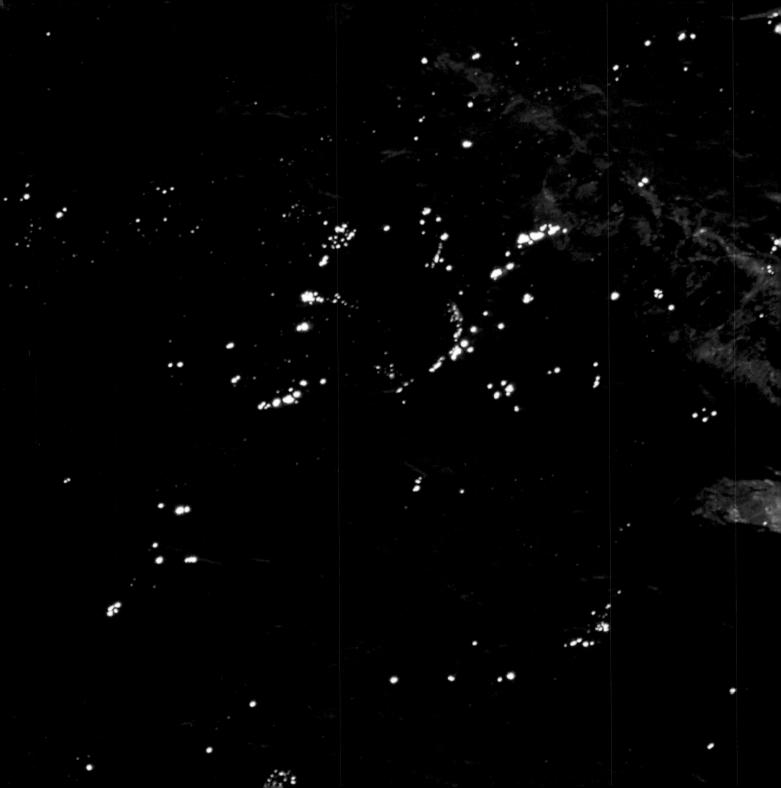

Some whales were once hunted nearly to extinction. Fortunately, the majority of people and their governments today wish to save and protect whales throughout the world. Someday, whales may cruise the sunny waves without harm from humans at all. That will be good news for whales and whale-lovers like you and me.

The whale dates back about 60 million years. They were members of a family of furry mammals that had 4 legs and a tail.

Some of these early mammals lived along the shores of swamps and estuaries where fresh water flowed into the sea. They probably walked along the beaches searching for food.

This right whale has some barnacles and crustaceans on its very large head.

Eventually, some began wading in the water in search of food. They would hold their breath to duck their heads under the water to gather food. As they waded deeper, they found more food. Soon some began to dive and swim in the shallows.

The longer they stayed at sea the better. The sea provided a plentiful supply of food. Over a long period of time they found that all their needs could be met in the sea. They had no reason to return to land. These land mammals evolved, over millions of years, into sea animals. They adapted to a new environment.

Once at sea they gradually took the shape of fish. Today, whales are so well adapted to life underwater that it is easy to forget they were once mammals of the land. Remember, this change from land life to sea life took place many millions of years ago.

Not all of these early mammals became sea mammals. Many survived well with the food available on land. In time they evolved into modern animals like the antelope, buffalo, caribou, cow, pig, moose, and musk-ox.

Probably the land mammal that is most closely related to the whale is the hippopotamus. It is surprising to think of the whale and hippopotamus as being related, but they are!

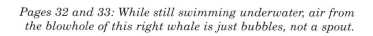

Pages 32 and 33: While still swimming underwater, air from the blowhole of this right whale is just bubbles, not a spout.

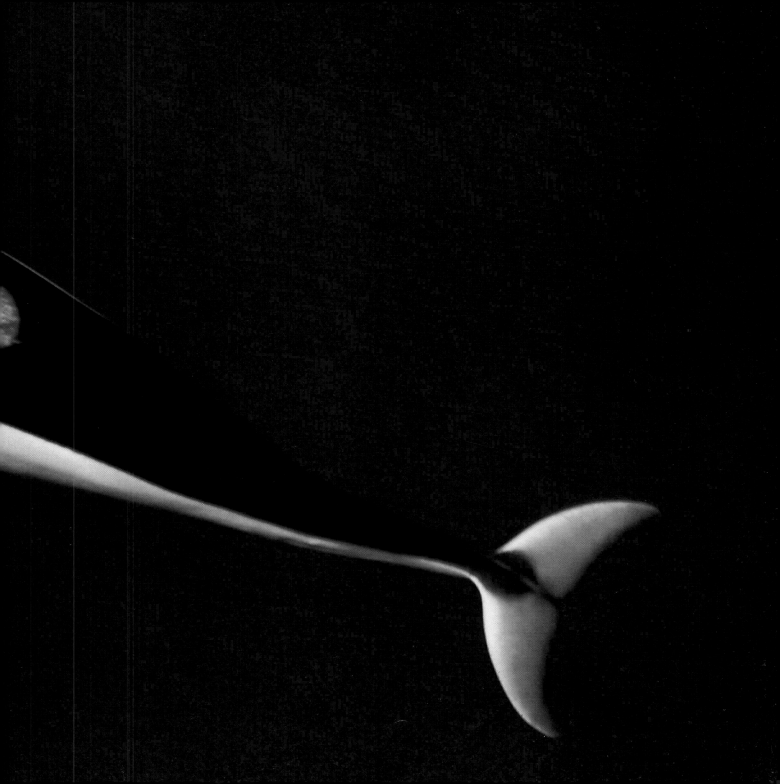

Some whales have teeth: they're called toothed whales. Some whales don't have teeth: they're called baleen whales.

Toothed whales eat fish and squid. Although they can hold their prey in their peg-like teeth, they swallow their food whole without chewing it. Some of them could easily swallow a person. Beluga whale, killer whale, narwhal whale, and sperm whale are examples of toothed whales.

Baleen whales are toothless. They eat plankton, which is a mixture of small sea animals and plants. They take in mouthfuls of plankton-filled water. Then the whale's tongue squeezes out the water, leaving only the nutritious plankton in its mouth. Blue whale, bowhead whale, fin whale, gray whale, humpback whale, right whale, and sei whale are examples of baleen whales.

Here is a list that will help you identify whales you might see swimming in the oceans of the world.

Beluga Whale

Maximum length: 16 feet
Weight: 1.5 tons (2,500 lbs.)
The beluga whale is white. It is often called the "sea canary" because of its loud bird-like chirping and whistling sounds. It has a very small head and no dorsal fin. The beluga whale has 34 teeth and 1 blowhole. It is found in the Arctic.

Blue Whale

Maximum length: 110 feet
Weight: 150 tons (300,000 lbs.)
The blue whale is the largest whale but it has a very small dorsal fin. It has 2 blowholes. The blue whale is bluish in color except for yellow on its underside caused by a coating of tiny water plants. It is found in all oceans.

Belugas are very easy to identify, with their pure white body.

Bowhead Whale
Maximum length: 55 feet
Weight: 45 tons (90,000 lbs.)
The bowhead whale looks very much like a right whale but it does not have a covering on its snout. It also does not have a dorsal fin but it has 2 blowholes. The bowhead whale is black with a white chin and is found in the Arctic.

Fin Whale
Maximum length: 82 feet
Weight: 100 tons (200,000 lbs.)
The fin whale has a fin on its back and a slender body. It has a gray-black back, a white underside, and a white patch on the front of its right jaw. Its left jaw is dark. The fin whale has 2 blowholes. It is found in all oceans.

Humpback Whale
Maximum length: 50 feet
Weight: 45 tons (90,000 lbs.)
The humpback whale gets its name from a humped roll of fat on its back. The humpback whale has many small marine animals like barnacles and crustaceans on its body. It has a small dorsal fin and 2 blowholes. Its large flippers can be 12 to 13 feet long. The humpback whale is dark in color with white flippers. It is found in all oceans.

When whales like this humpback push straight up out of the water to get a look around, it is called "spyhopping."

Killer Whale

Maximum length: 30 feet

Weight: 10 tons (20,000 lbs.)

The killer whale has a glossy black back and a white underside. It has a very tall dorsal fin and 1 blowhole. It has 40 to 48 teeth, and has a ferocious reputation. The killer whale has also been called the orca whale. It is found in all oceans but especially in cold regions.

Gray Whale

Maximum length: 60 feet

Weight: 40 tons (80,000 lbs.)

The gray whale has a low ridge on its back in place of a fin. It has 2 blowholes. It is dark gray or black with many white spots and barnacles on its head. The gray whale is found in the north Pacific.

Two of the killer whale's body markings are called its "eyepatch" and its "saddle."

Narwhal Whale

Maximum length: 18 feet
Weight: 2 tons (4,000 lbs.)
The male narwhal whale has 3 teeth plus a spiral ivory tusk about 8 feet long jutting from the left side of its head. The female has no tusk. The narwhal has 1 blowhole but no dorsal fin. The narwhal is gray-white with dark gray or black spots on its skin and is found in the Arctic.

Right Whale

Maximum length: 60 feet
Weight: 50 tons (100,000 lbs.)
The right whale has a rough covering on its snout and a very large head. It has 2 blowholes but no dorsal fin. It has short, broad flippers and swims slowly. The right whale is black with some white on its chin and belly. It is found in all oceans.

In the arctic springtime, narwhals swim in cracks in the ice to breathe.

Sei Whale

Maximum length: 55 feet
Weight: 40 tons (80,000 lbs.)
The sei whale looks very similar to a fin whale, but it has no white patch on its jaw. Like the fin whale, it also has a fin on its back and 2 blowholes. The sei whale has a dark back and a light underside. It is found in all oceans.

Sperm Whale

Maximum length: 65 feet
Weight: 60 tons (120,000 lbs.)
The sperm whale has 1 blowhole and a hump on its back but no dorsal fin. It has 35 to 65 teeth. Its enormous head makes up a third of the body length. The head contains a large amount of "spermaceti," a waxy material used in some cosmetics. The sperm whale is dark gray and is found in all oceans.

Pages 46 and 47: Sperm whales can stay underwater for over an hour.

Because the sei whale has no teeth, it must teach its calf to catch and eat plankton.

Other titles available in our popular

WILDLIFE *For Kids* SERIES™

See your nearest bookseller
or order by phone 1-800-328-3895

NORTHWORD
NORTHWORD PRESS